it's wings
that make
birds fly

Sandra Weiner

it's wings that make birds fly

The Story of a Boy

Pantheon Books

IT'S WINGS THAT MAKE BIRDS FLY—a story based on the
experiences and feelings of a Negro boy and his friends
—emerged from Sandra Weiner's taped conversations
with them.

*For my daughter Dore
and to the memory of
Dan and Otis*

Otis Bennett's world is one of grubby store fronts and trash-filled alleys. But it is a world in which a few people manage to make things good for him. ''I likes people,'' he says. ''I likes my sisters, my brothers. I likes my father and grandmother. I likes my mother and my cousins and my aunt.''

Otis is ten years old. It would be wonderful if he still likes people ten years from now—wonderful, too, if people still like him. But by then he will be a man, a black man, with grown-up black man thoughts about ugly store fronts and alleys; about what is good or bad. What seems like fun for him at ten might be tragedy to him at twenty. I hope a lot of things for Otis. I hope that he will be allowed to grow up straight. I hope that he will be allowed to realize the promise that is inside him, and many other ten-year-old boys like him. And I hope that we, you and I, will come to know our responsibility toward helping Otis into a manhood of dignity.

Gordon Parks

My name is Otis Bennett or Peewee or Junior. I was born in a hospital in New York City. My birthday is June 19, no—29, 1958. Right now I live with my father and his mother, my Grandma Bennett. My father, he's got a store with ice cream, soda pop, and hot dogs. My father and mother, they don't get along so good so they don't live in the same house no more. Sometimes I go visit my mother. She lives downtown with some of my other brothers and sisters.

I likes people. I likes my sisters, my brothers. I likes my father and grandmother. I likes my mother and my cousins and my aunt.

My Grandma Bennett, she takes care of us and cleans our clothes. She buys me shoes and pants and shirts, and she's gonna buy me another notebook cause this one is all out. She's gonna buy me one of these big notebooks, hardback.

This grandmother, she hits me only when I do things

that are wrong. Not hard, just a slap across the face. She worked hard for twenty years in a big fancy hotel and she says she's sorry they're tearing it down cause she don't have to work no more. She used to meet all kinds of people down there. Now she works for a lady downtown east, but she's getting too old to work too much.

She keeps everything nice and clean. The minute you puts paper on the floor she makes you pick it up, and they'll be the one that mops the floor, and whoever be the one that is standing up on the couch, they be the one that cleans the couch, cause she spends all her time cleaning the house.

I used to live with my other grandmother, Grandma Mitchell, my mother's mother. My brother Albert—we call him Trigger—he also lived with her and my half-sister, Ellie Lou. At first it was nice living with Grandma Mitchell, but later on she got so mean I didn't like her no more. I got up one morning and my Grandmother Mitchell said, "Junior, where is your homework?" So I told her my teacher said I had to remember in my head what I did in the classroom. So then she hit me with a stick and I cried.

I waited for Ellie Lou in the yard in school that day and I said, "Do you want to go to our mother?" And she said "Yeah," so we went. We followed the 39 bus and

when it got lost we followed the other 39 bus. When we got to the bridge I saw a fish hop right out the water. I said, ''Ellie Lou, look at the fish,'' and she threw a rock and it hit the water.

When we got to my mother's house on 123rd Street she said, ''You have to go back, that's where you belong, with your grandmother. I've got your other sisters and brothers.'' So my Grandma Mitchell she came and got Ellie Lou, but I stayed cause I didn't want to go back.

At night my mother went to work and I took care of the babies. The babies is called Harlan and Harold and they're twins and they're ten months old. Annie Lou, my mother, she showed me how you push over the diaper cause it's too big for the baby. One of them he cried and I gave him milk in his bottle. I likes to be there. The fat baby, he eats fast and he smiles a lot. I likes the babies.

When my mother came home she gave me some money and I bought cookies and potato chips. One baby had a tooth so I gave him a cookie and the other baby he was sleeping so I left one on the television for him.

On Thursday Grandma Mitchell came and she took me back, and my mother said she shouldn't beat me so hard. I was glad to see my sister and Trigger. But a

few days later Grandma Mitchell she beat me so hard I ran out and I didn't have too much clothes on me. When I got downstairs the tears were over my eyes and it was cold and I ain't had no coat on. There was a super there that I liked and he liked me and I know him, so he took me in his house and he gave me a belt and a pair of pants and he said, where do I want to go. I said, ''I want to go to my father's,'' so he gave me twenty cents cause I ain't seen my father in a long while. The super, he likes me cause me and Trigger helped him put out the garbage. I said, ''Thank you, I appreciate very much,'' and he said, ''You be scattin off to your father.'' He gave me an old jacket to wear with the pants.

I took the 39 bus uptown to Fort Henry. When I got to my father's store I looked in and there were lots of men. Then I saw a man and I said, ''That can't be Otis!''—except now I call him Pop—and he said ''Junior'' and I said ''Hi.'' He gave me a hamburger and played the record machine and we danced.

Later we went to my Grandmother Bennett's house and she was glad to see me. She gave me syrup and biscuits and it was so good. She said, do I want some more, and I said, ''I sure do want some more.'' I told them that Grandma Mitchell had hit me with a stick. They said, ''Well, we're going to see about that next week,'' so they went to see about it next week.

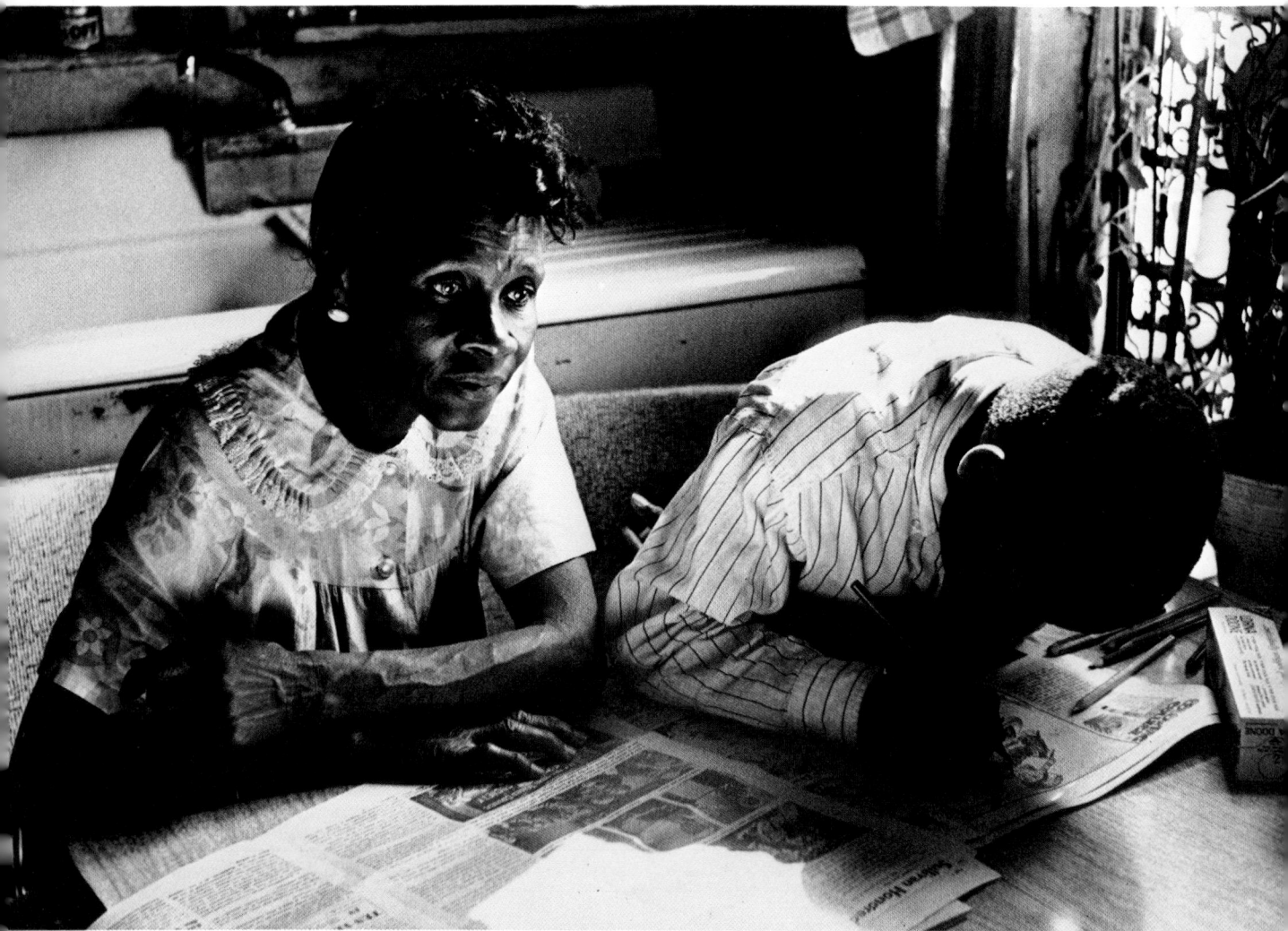

Now at Grandma Bennett's I do my homework when I come home and I can not go outside until I finish, and I don't care if it takes eight o'clock or all night but I finish my work as quick as possible and it better be right. My Grandmother Bennett, she looks at it, nobody else in the house to do it. I'm upstairs doing it and my father he's out working.

My grandmother does the cooking the easiest way, like the shake and bake. Yesterday we had potato salad, meat, peas, and rice. And she cooks a cake every Saturday and I get around five pieces. Her cake is so good I could eat a million pieces. She makes designs on the cakes like a house and girls and boys playing.

Now I'm living with Grandma Bennett I goes to a different school. There are twenty-six children in my fourth grade. I can't say the teacher's name yet. She got a hard name like Baffenther, but she knows my name.

My teacher in the other school, Mister Healey, he was nasty. Mister Healey, he was fat and he ain't got too much hair on his head. Even when they didn't follow the reading a few minutes, Mister Healey hits people, and then he said, ''You gonna be good, you gonna be good.''

Rick was my best friend in that school, and Aaron and Manuela were my friends. She is Spanish and speaks a little English. I can only speak in Spanish from one to I don't know what. I couldn't get time to know all the kids in my class because Grandma Mitchell she always made me come home at twelve o'clock. I come home to eat my lunch and then I have to wait till it's time to go back to the classroom, and all the time I got

is just to do my work. Well, my Grandmother Mitchell she didn't want me to be mixing with other company cause I might get in trouble.

Maybe you can get into bad company and do bad things and you may follow them and do what they do. That's what I used to do when I was in Mister Healey's class. Some of the children was older, some are me. These bad company, they was in the other school. One of these boys, Joseph, he always liked to make trouble for everybody. If somebody is in the classroom that he likes and they start messing and punching you and you hit 'em back, then Joseph he jumps in and wants to fight too and makes some trouble. He's not too big, but he's bigger. He threatened me a lot of time, but I don't pay him no mind. He picks on me cause he gots a lot of friends in Mister Healey's class.

Sometimes the big kids beat me up just because I'm helping my brother or sister. You see, my brother he got in a lot of trouble and then he come running to me and he says, "Junior! Junior! They gonna beat me up." So he jump behind me and I gets in front of him and then he start running and I takes up for him. My sister, she don't fight much.

But now I have a lady in the new school. Mrs. Baffenther, she's about my Grandmother Bennett's size. She knows my name. I didn't know fractions the first day I went

there, but the second day and the third day when I went I still didn't know my fractions. Then me and her went out the back table and me and her did fractions together and now I like to do fractions. Now I know how to do my fractions and the cups, like how many cups in a pint. I know all of that. Sometimes I'm good at spelling, but I have to learn more and I don't know my division and I don't know how to write or read so good.

In school now I like Robert, Sharon, Keith—and once Sharon took me to her house. On Halloween we had a party and one kid came as a boy with a notebook. My Grandmother gave me a mask. But I wouldn't wear it cause she gave me a devil. I don't like the devil cause he's always bothering people and disturbing them and making noise. At the party Sharon brought her sister from the third grade and we played put the tail on the donkey. They eyefold me and pushed me around three times and then I walked to the donkey, and if the desk got in your way they moved it and so I put the tail on his head.

And we played the music with the chairs. And all the children would move around the chairs until they stopped the music and then everyone looked for a chair. Then the winner is when there are two people and one chair, and the guy who gets the chair, and the other guy he get the music.

I like to read *Happiness Hill,* the book from school. It tells about the man who was going to hunt a skunk and then he went out there and caught the skunk and shot him. Then he ran in the house and put on some other clothes, it smelled so bad. One of these days he's gonna shoot a deer, but he missed the deer and shot the tree. Then he said he'll get him a bear. He missed the bear, the bear tried to catch him. He ran into the house and said, I'll better eat some oatmeal.

I also read *Jonathan Bing.* He gets up early one morning and he goes downstairs and hollers ''Good morning'' and nobody answers. He looks all over the room and he don't see nobody. So all the furniture's gone and the fire put out and no breakfast on the table. So he goes outside and he sees the pig hollering too, and he says, ''I'm hungry.'' Then he went to the geese and they were hollering too, and he said to them, ''What are you hollering for?'' They said, ''I'm hungry.'' He went on down by the river and he saw his mother coming back for him. He said, ''Why did you have to leave without me? I wanted to help with the furniture too.'' Then they said they were going to catch the pig, and one of them had to hold the pig and the other drive the wagon.

My favorite story is *Hansel and Gretel.* But best of all I like Tarzan. He likes to take care of animals. I likes animals. I likes puppies and rabbits. Soft and nice color, playful.

SALE OR RENT
25 x 100
HARRISON
Fl. 6-8930

CLOSED
BETWEEN
1 & 2 P.M.

One day I was bringing home my rabbit, my black-and-white one. A man gave him to me. He lives around the corner. He likes me and he gave him to me, but he died. The man didn't die, the rabbit died. I was coming out the door and these big teenagers they was there and they started throwing bricks at him and smashed him. I fed him carrots and lettuce and I gave him celery. I put the celery in my pocket and he gets up on the couch and he takes it out of my pocket.

I'm trying real hard to be good in school, do all my homework, and be faithful. I even got a glove as a prize for being good. My teacher gave it to me. Now I got a bat too, and I can play ball outside with the other kids. Sometimes Mrs. Baffenther, my teacher, she gets mad and screams when I don't listen. And she sends me to the principal's office to get straightened out. I likes my principal. Then I promise to do what I am told, to be in the classroom on time, and I won't be hanging around in the halls.

One time we learned about Marco Polo, Christopher Columbus, and the Vikings and the Indians. One thing got me confused. They said Christopher Columbus discovered America. But then I heard the Vikings discovered it. The whole class went to visit the Indian Museum and they had a big totem pole outside but you wasn't allowed to climb it. These Indians, they was colored red men.

We was studying about the Statue of Liberty and Mrs. Baffenther said we would take a day off and visit her if the children promised to behave right. That morning my Grandmother Bennett she gave me a ham sandwich and money to buy a soda pop. My father, he gave me money to buy a Statue of Liberty. We took a long subway ride and when we got out at the Bowling Green I could smell the water. We didn't have too much time, and we saw the ferry and everybody started running, but by the time we got there the gangplank was up and the boat was moving and we had to wait for the next boat. When the boat began to move I was scared. I stood close to Carmela, a girl in my class, and I wasn't so scared no more.

When it was time to get off I asked my teacher if we were here, cause I couldn't see no statue. The boat was full of people—Chinese children from the other schools. Mrs. Baffenther said this was the island, Bedloe Island, where the Statue of Liberty sat. So we walked around her, we even went in her. I looked out a window from her and my friend George looked out another window. We had lunch like a picnic near the water. We sang "This Old Man" and danced. I asked Mrs. Baffenther if this was the Hudson River. She said, "Yes, plus another river." When we were inside we looked for the poem Mrs. Baffenther told about by Mrs. Lazarus, and then we looked for the man who carved her, Mister Bartholdi.

I bought a statue of her that's a pencil sharpener for my brother and a post card of her for my grandmother and a pencil for my father.

On the way back it was a long ride so we told jokes and sang. I told:

What did the Indian say when his dog fell in the fire?
Hot Dog!

What did the man say when he threw his clock out the window?
He wanted to see time fly.

What did the little firecracker say to the big firecracker?
I can blow up better than you.

What did the little hand say to the big hand?
Move over, I'll be over in an hour.

Why did the moron salute the refrigerator?
Because it was General Electric.

What did the old lady do with all the apples when she had eight apples and ten kids?
She made applesauce.

The Sport of Kings has returned to Queens.

Big A.

After I ran away I used to feel lonely for Trigger. I took the 39 bus back to the old house to see him. He was standing on the street, crying, with Grandma Mitchell.

I asked him, "Why are you crying?" and so he said, "I lost my tablet and my hat." Grandma Mitchell said to me, "You're trying to make trouble between me and Trigger. Just get away and go back to your father." I said, "Uh, uh, I ain't trying to make no trouble, I just see Trigger crying." And she said, "Uh, uh, Trigger ain't crying." He was crying all right, and he told me if he didn't find the tablet and hat he was going to get a beating. She said she didn't want Trigger to be close to me, but he was close to me.

The next morning she hit Trigger with the stick and he ran out the house. We was wondering when Trigger would have faith and courage to run away, and next thing I know my father he called and he said that Trigger was at his store. I was so glad he finally ran away.

He said after Grandma Mitchell hit him he ran out the house and the same super that helped me helped him. He gave him twenty cents like he did me, and Trigger found the way to the store. He wasn't sure where it was, because he was little then when we first was there. I was bigger than him. I was eight and he was seven and I knew my way from Grandma Mitchell's to Otis's store.

Then my father and Trigger came to Grandma Bennett's house and she gave us syrup and biscuits again and we wanted it again and again, and we had three times syrup and biscuits. Then she and my father they talked while we colored in the newspapers, and my grandmother said she thought it would be just fine if Trigger stayed with us.

Now my brother's here I don't have to be alone all the time and me and him can play together. I don't have to be afraid of the dark cause I sleep in the same bed with my brother. Trigger says he's glad he's with me now and close to me, cause a brother should be close to a brother. Sometimes Trigger he gets angry at me and I gets angry at him and we don't talk to each other for a couple of minutes, and then we'll be talking to each other.

One night we was all watching the TV and we saw this picture about this lady. She got married and her husband

wanted to go and fight for America, so he got shot in the leg first and then in the chest and he died. It was in Korea that he went to fight and got shot, and he stayed alive for two more days. Then the lady she started crying. When they brought her husband from the hospital she kissed him and they had a funeral. She got married with another man with a mustache.

Sometimes when we ain't watching the TV we play records and dance. One time we was playing in the park. We took a long hike to the other end and my brother he felt like singing. He knows best ''Stop! In the Name of Love,'' so he sang that one. Wherever I go I feels like dancing, even when I'm down. I likes my music. To my opinion I'm a good dancer.

My father, he likes to dance, but most of all he likes to play punch. Punching somebody like working on a punching bag. I don't mind him doing it to me, and he lets me punch him back so I can learn to fight for myself. He says he's glad his boys are back with him cause that's where they belong, with their father. He's gonna buy me and Trigger some maroon bikes.

One time a boy downstairs made trouble and took our ball and bat away and my father came down and told him to leave us alone, and the boy got so big and smart my father had to hit him. And he said he was gonna get his father, and my father said, ''You can get your

father, your mother, your sister, and anybody else you want, just don't play with these kids smaller than you."

Once I hit a ball that went over a boy's head and down a cellar. He said to me, "You hit it, so you can get it," so I went down there and I got it. Sometimes we play stickball with a tin can so it don't break windows or go up the roof. I can knock it to the corner of the next street in between them garbage cans. When it gets hot from playing we open the hydrant, and if you puts a tin can on the nozzle of the hydrant it makes a big waterfall and you cools off and you see a rainbow until the cops come and shuts it off.

Now I have a new friend, Susan. She lives in my building on the second floor and her friend she lives downstairs across the hall. A boy that sits next to me in school he don't like me, so I said to him, "Well, I ain't asking you to like me." I don't want to like people who don't like me, no way. I have to sit with him cause the teacher told me to sit with him. He says I don't take a bath and all that, which I do. Today I took a bath, but tomorrow I'm gonna skip. That's what I do every day from now on. I takes a quick bath in the morning. I said to him, "Boy, I'm sure you don't take a bath," and the way he smell he sure must not don't.

This apartment is not a very pretty building. I'd like to live across the street or a block or two up. When it's

cold like last night Trigger and I gets into bed and he puts his legs on my legs and I said, ''Don't, your legs are cold, move them,'' and then I puts my feet on his feet and he told me to move my feet. Someday maybe we can live in a good building like other peoples do.

I used to like my Grandmother Mitchell. She tried her best to learn us something so when we grow up we would be a Jehovah Witness like her. That's what I used to hope to do, and go to Bethel where you study. My brother, he wanted to go to Bethel too. We went to the Kingdom Hall on 136th Street. It's a small place, and on Tuesday night we'd go to Miss Smith's house and then Thursday we'd go to Kingdom Hall and on Wednesday we'd have our personal study with Mister Laurence.

I wanted to be a Jehovah Witness like my Grandma Mitchell cause they're honest and love God and the Bible. I used to sell *The Watchtower* and *Awake* and I'd say to people, "My name is Otis Bennett and I have *The Watchtower* and *Awake* here, which is very interesting and it's only a small contribution of fifteen cents." I sold fourteen one Sunday and sixteen another, cause I went to this building down the block and knocked at all the doors. And then when I got home my grandmother she said, "Junior, that ain't your territory."

DEVOTION

Sometimes in Kingdom Hall I'll be thinking what I'm gonna tell the children in my school. I'd tell them God in the heaven is Jehovah God. They say he ain't. They say that God and Mary is up there too. I say Mary ain't up there. There's only one God up there and maybe a lot of people that call themselves gods. Sometimes when I wouldn't be telling the truth I know he'll be punishing me. After Armageddon. But there are ways if you are telling stories to somebody they'll wind up knowing that you're telling stories.

One Summer we went to Baltimore for a Jehovah Convention and we had a hard time getting someplace to live for the four days. Because some people don't like Jehovah Witnesses. We went to one lady she lived far up someplace, and it cost two dollars to her house and two dollars back. Cause we used to go to a meeting at the ball park. So we went back to the ball park and they said they knew a lady who lived near there but she was at work so we had to wait and when she came home again we stayed with her four days.

I'd like to go back to Baltimore cause when you get up in the morning you have toast-ups and every morning while we're asleep the lady comes in and sits on my bed and she tells us, "Come on, get up and go get out of bed and wash up and come get ready to eat." Sometimes she let us eat on the porch where it was sunny and warm.

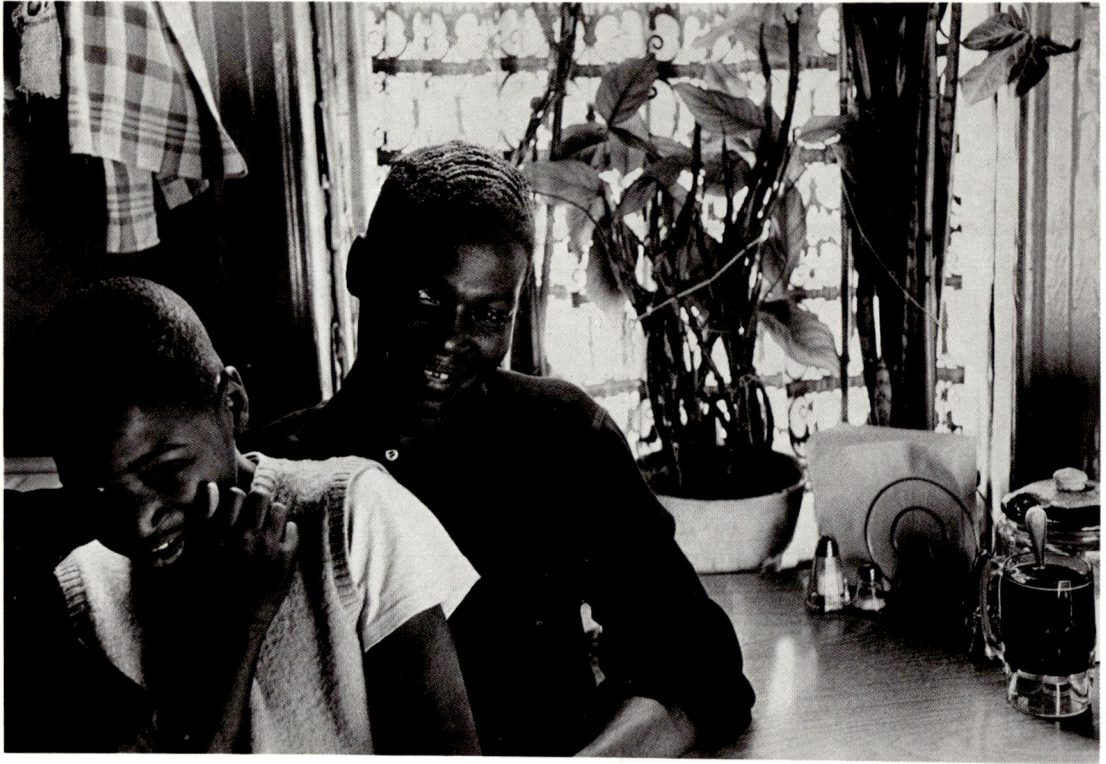

I still remember the story of Eve and Adam from my Bible study. Eve was in the evil garden and the snake spoke to her, and the devil and the snake told Eve to eat the food, but God told her if she eat the food she'll positively die, but Satan got the snake to tell her that she will positively not die, she will be like God and know good and bad. So she took the food and she ate the food and she gave Adam some of the food and they both had sin.

Since I moved to Grandma Bennett's I don't have to be a Jehovah Witness no more. I don't know what I'm gonna be now. I'm gonna start attending church, but I don't know what church yet. My father, he don't go to church cause he has to work all day Sunday and Saturday too. One night before I was going to bed he said, "Shake my hand, Junior," so I took his hand and he squeezed mine real tight and I said, "Well, good night." So now I wait for him to come home from work so I can shake his hand. Sometimes he squeezes my hand so hard it hurts, but I don't cry.

Sometimes I have scary dreams. I see monsters, big dinosaurs. Like it's someplace in the jungle in Africa, and me and the dinosaur comes and I get crushed and then I keep on going. I dreamed about a dragon. He was tall and got a long tail, sharp teeth, and he got these sticky things sticking in back of his head and going all the way down his back, and he got a mouth that fire comes out of.

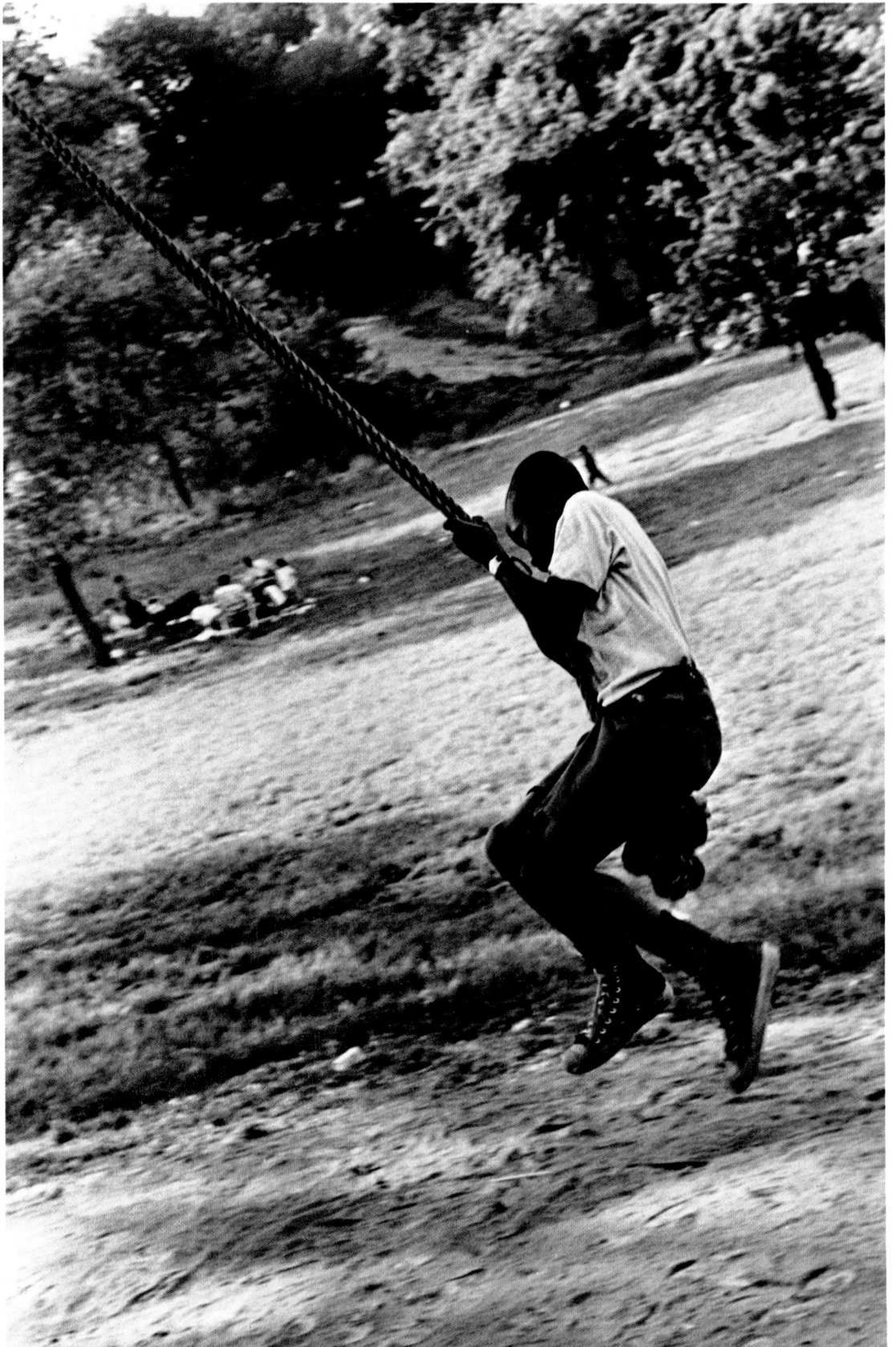

I don't daydream but my brother do. Sometimes when I'm in school I'd like to be outside throwing snowballs. Sometimes in the spring I feel like going swimming. At first I wasn't a good swimmer, but I went to the pool and didn't exactly jump off the diving board but I jumped off the edge. Now I can jump off the diving board.

I heard about Africa in school and sometimes I look at Tarzan in the African jungle. I like Tarzan because he likes to save animals and he likes people. Once the whole class went to the Zoo and we saw these yaks, a whole family with lots of baby yaks. We also went to the Natural Museum where we saw the animals you didn't have a chance to see in real life.

I don't want to go up in a space ship. I know why I don't want to go up in space—cause if the ship go out of order I'll land on the moon and never get off. I hope I never go up in an airplane. When I gets up there I'm gonna want to get down, cause up there I'm scared.

When I grow up I'd like to be an ice cream man cause a lot of children like ice cream. I'd like to be a doctor cause I can help people, and I'd like to be a bus driver cause a bus driver he knows where he's going and a lot of people come onto his bus.

If I had a supermarket I'd have me to sell cooked ham and lettuce on a hard roll in cellophane in the cold sec-

tion. And I'd also have a place where eating-things can stay warm so when nobody's home you don't have to cook it.

I'll tell you one thing about myself. One time my brother and my Grandmother Bennett were together and I was all alone and had my books and had my brother's books and I was in the park. My grandmother and Trigger went to do some business and I was playing alone and I sang songs and all of that, then I look around and nobody to play with. So I sang another song and finally while I was singing I saw my grandmother and I was crying, but before she came close I wiped my tears. Lonely feels like sitting in a dark room all by yourself.

There's a song that I always sing to my brother:

A bird in the tree he's beautiful to look at as you.
The bird in the tree he came to you and you came
to me.

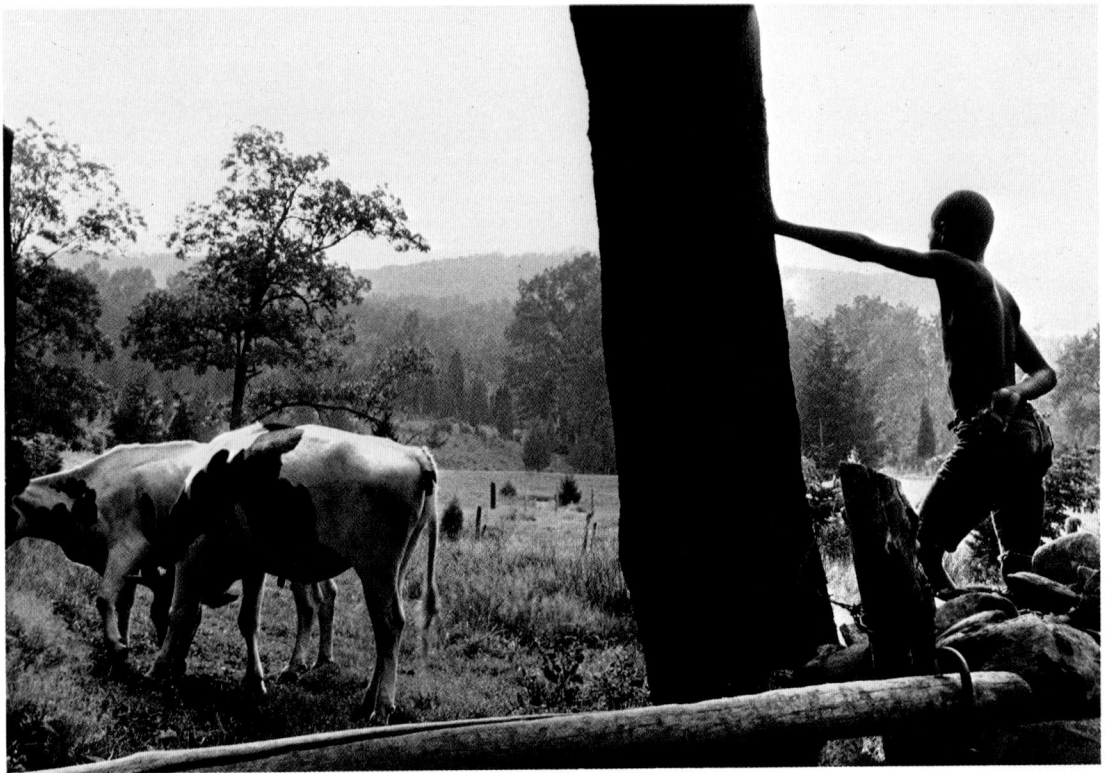

T his summer I went to camp. It's not really a camp, it's a private home on a green hill in Pennsylvania. It's a whole family. Mom and Dad, and Polly, Hope, and William, and Grandma and Grandpa. It's a Fresh Air Family.

I like going to Grandma and Grandpa. They live near the lake and you can go fishing. I call them Mom and Dad and Grandpa and Grandma. One time I caught a fish flying in the air, a big fish. Grandpa caught four. Polly, she was too fat and she was afraid she'd fall overboard, and she only caught one and every time she put a worm on the hook she'd pull it up and nothing on the hook. She was taking all the bait.

At the Andrews' they have dogs, rabbits, cats, frogs. I heard frogs at night chirping, and the crickets. I would rather live in the country because I likes animals and there's lots of animals in the country.

They had a bathroom upstairs and downstairs and a lot

of rooms. At first I was scared of the Andrews' dog. I felt fine until I met the dog, then I was afraid of him until they told me he wouldn't bite. He was a friendly dog. Next day when I came out he came out too. When I walked down the aisle, I mean path, he barked and I jumped in front of Mrs. Andrews. I call her Mom. The dog's name is Queenie but in the house we call him Queenbee.

Mister Andrews—I call him Dad—he goes to work, but he also works on the farm with the animals. He milks the cows and lets us ride on the back of the truck down the path where he parks his truck. Once I tried to milk a cow. She was the first cow I ever saw in person. She was black and white. I got the milk from her and I gave it to the calf. I won't drink milk straight from the cow.

Grandma and Grandpa Andrews, they put a rope up in the tree and we used to swing around the tree like we was Tarzan, and we used to jump in the bushes and see these light-bugs at night. One time William he was going to Grandma's house, he saw a snake going across the bridge and he came back and told us and told Mom and Dad.

And Grandma she also has a dog. One day in the rain Grandma Andrews caught a bird that was sick. It almost died but they picked it up and brought it into the house and fed it. They fed it plums—that's what it likes, plums.

I seen birds too. Sometimes I'd be in the barn with the chickens and I'd be hiding, and these little birds would come in and they couldn't find their way back up, and then I used to pick them up and they'd go all over the window and try to get out, and then I'd pick them up two at a time and take them back to Mom and put them in a cage, and later on I'd set them free. One time a frog that don't live in water, it was under the house, so I picked it up and put it in my hand and I told Grandma Andrews. She said, "Don't let it leak on you, cause if it leaks on you you'll get warts on your hands."

On rainy days we'd stay upstairs. William, he got a big train track with nineteen cars. I never ain't seen such a long track. We always used to go down to the woods and there are a lot of apples on the tree over us and we'd pick them and make apple bombs. If we eat them we get all blowed up. Sometimes we just go down in the field and pick blueberries and sometimes we used to eat them wild. And Mom would make jam and a syrup with them, and jelly. Next time I'll bring some home. One time I bought VO-5 and a roll of hair curlers as a present for my Grandmother Bennett.

Maybe I'd like to be a farmer. I want to go back to the country. The cows and the frogs and the rabbits they likes me. They played with me just like they played with Polly, Hope, and William.

I like the fall now and on a warm day I can hear the birds. They be on my fire escape. I gets up and open the window and they fly up to me right on the sixth floor and they starts singing. And I just look at them making bird music. I seen them brown and gray and a little blue.

I know where lots of pigeons is and I try to catch them but they too quick. I go to the park and one day a baby squirrel I was trying to catch went all the way up the tree. I went after it and the next thing I knew there was a nest and it was a girl squirrel. The nest was a hole something like a bird's nest, but it wasn't round. A hole in the tree, and it got things like straw and leaves and there were baby squirrels in it that couldn't see yet, and she was rounding up nuts for them. And I didn't want to bother the girl squirrel. I knew it was a girl because she was getting ready to have another one, cause of her stomach, it was fat. Better not for me to bother her.

Then I saw a boy squirrel. I knew it was a boy because

it was guarding the nest. I chased it up the tree and it ran to the lady squirrel and I said, ''That's a whole family, I ain't gonna bother with them.'' I found a teeny squirrel and chased it up the tree. The kids with me yelled, ''Don't catch it! Don't catch it!'' and I said I wasn't gonna have it for a pet. They said animals should have freedom. I said, ''Oh yeah, I forgot about that.'' Animals should be free and I let the thing go. Then I ran up after it again, but I only wanted to see it go back to the mother squirrel.

I think a lot about the birds in the trees. I once caught a bird. It fell out the tree and I caught it in my hands. I climbed the tree to return it to its nest and there were four more birds up there and the mother and father was gone.

My Grandmother Bennett, she likes her bird Skippy and she plays with him. Sometimes she takes him out the cage and he sings and she sings.

It's wings that make birds fly. If I had me a pair of wings I'd fly out the window, and people would look up at the sky and say, ''Why there's Superman,'' and I'd be so proud. But then I'd be tired staying up there and want to come down and couldn't. And then someone shot up at me and people saw me falling and they said, ''Why that ain't Superman, that's a dead, dead, dead, long gone boy.''

Shortly after this story was written, the young boy whose life it largely portrays was killed in an accident while playing in the street.

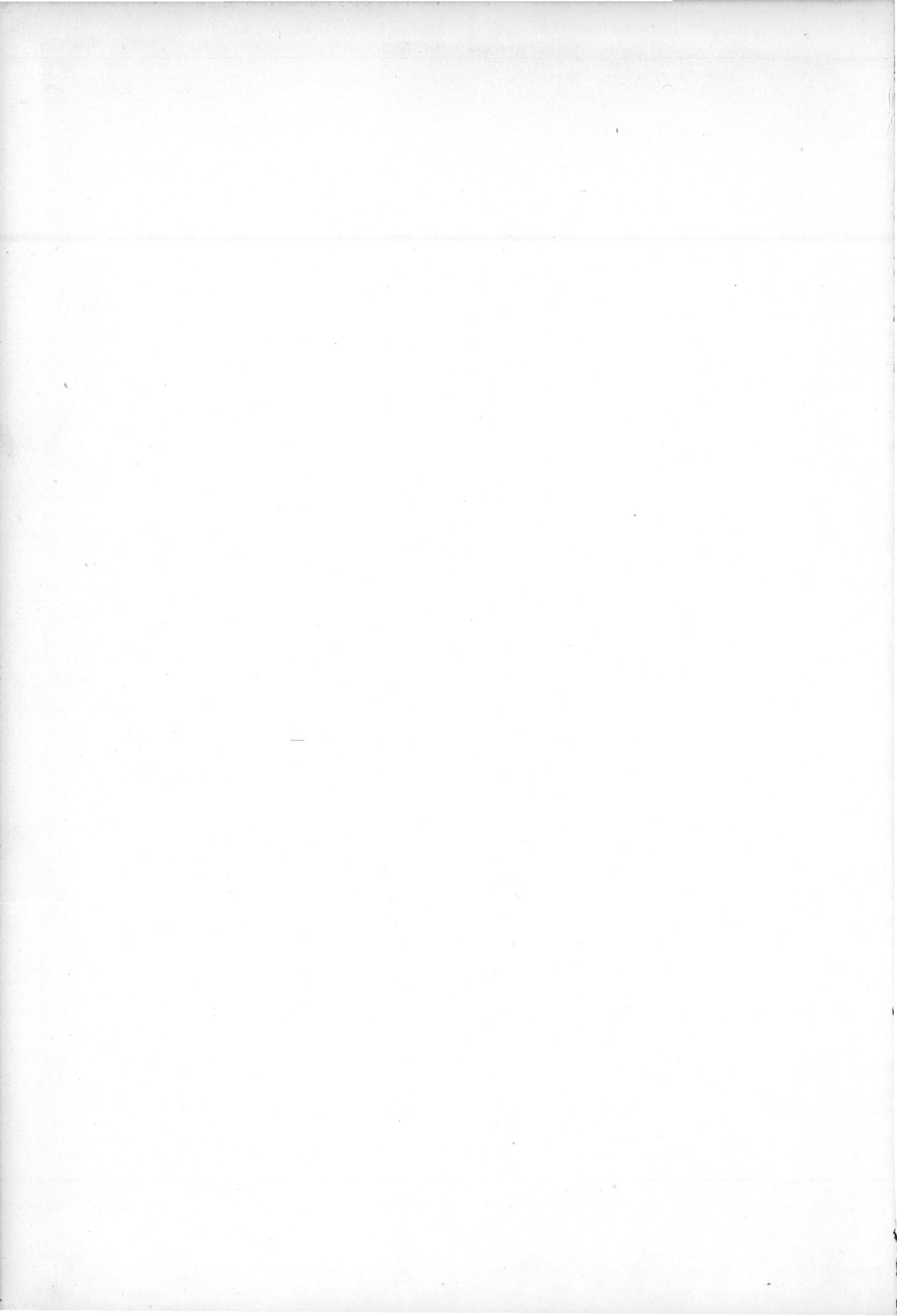